me Six
Intermediate

Accent on
GILLOCK

by William Gillock

CONTENTS

ISBN 978-0-87718-081-4

WILLIS MUSIC

EXCLUSIVELY DISTRIBUTED BY

HAL•LEONARD®

Visit Hal Leonard Online at
www.halleonard.com

World headquarters, contact:
Hal Leonard
7777 West Bluemound Road
Milwaukee, WI 53213
Email: info@halleonard.com

In Europe, contact:
Hal Leonard Europe Limited
42 Wigmore Street
Marylebone, London, W1U 2RN
Email: info@halleonardeurope.com

In Australia, contact:
Hal Leonard Australia Pty. Ltd.
4 Lentara Court
Cheltenham, Victoria, 3192 Australia
Email: info@halleonard.com.au

To the Metairie Senior Music Club

Adagio Esotico

William Gillock

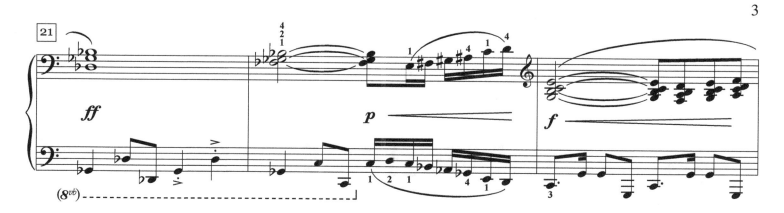

Baghdad

William Gillock

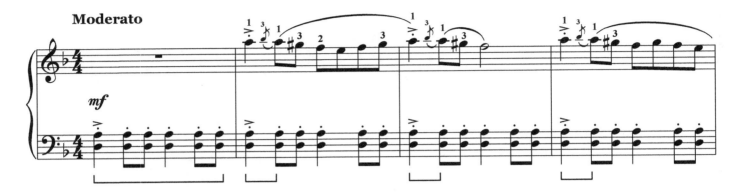

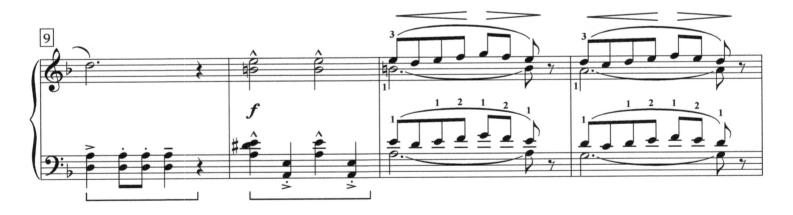

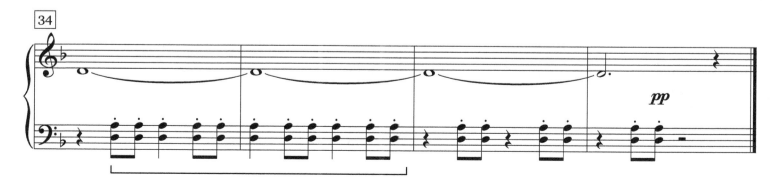

By a Sylvan Lake

William Gillock

With a slow, languid motion

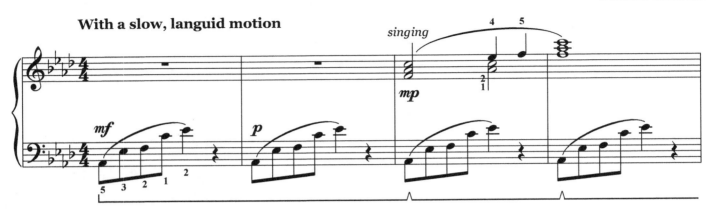

To Mrs. Charles N. Turner

A Woodland Legend

William Gillock

Slowly, with much freedom

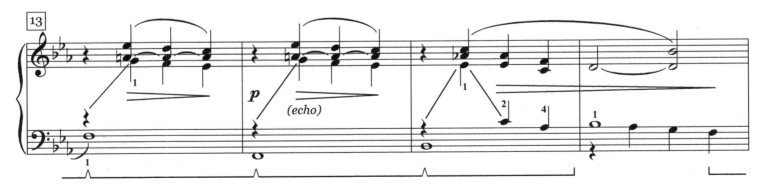

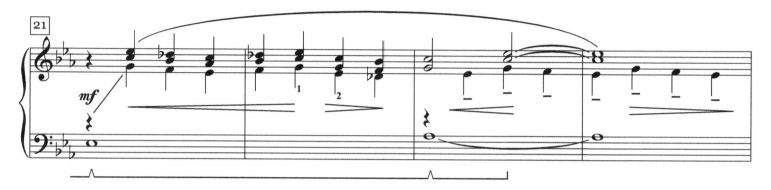

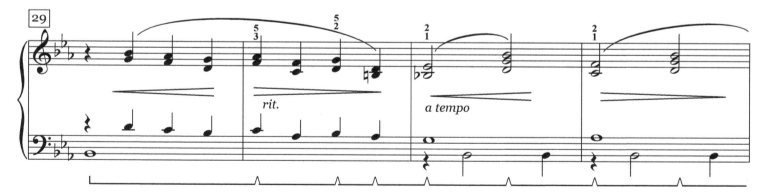

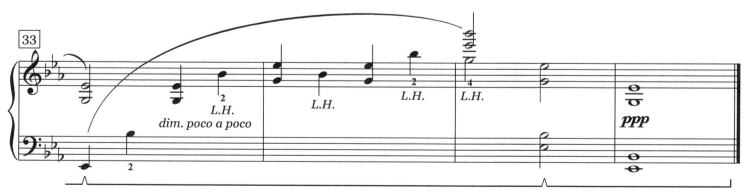

Viennese Rondo

(Homage to Josef Strauss)

William Gillock

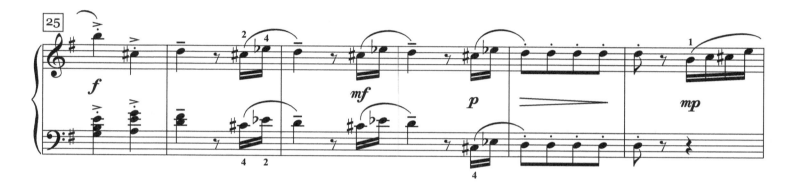

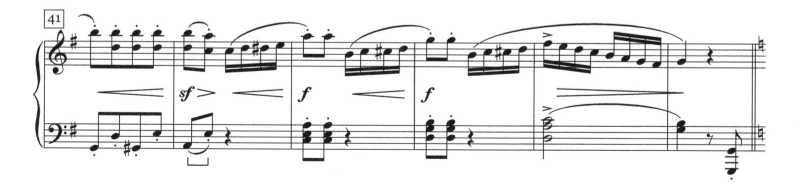

Fountain in the Rain

William Gillock

Gently flowing ♩ = ca. 88

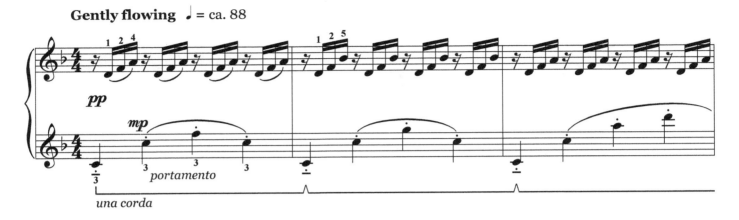

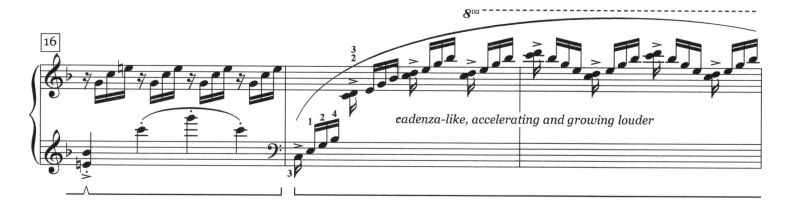

cadenza-like, accelerating and growing louder

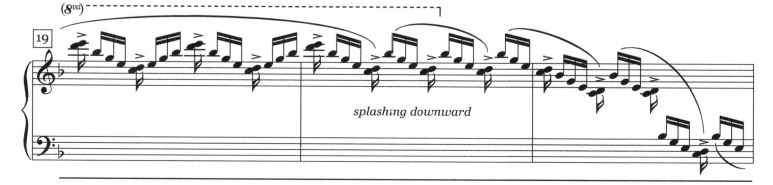

splashing downward

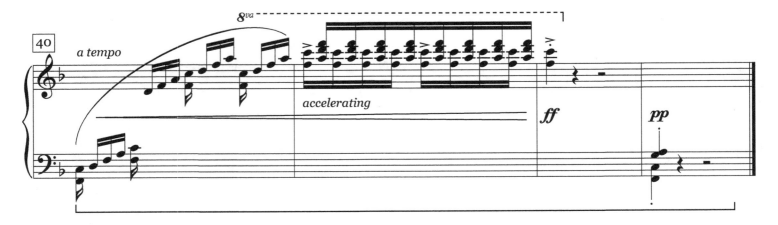